W9-AZW-534

Gun Education and Safety

GUNS & AMMUNITION

BRIAN KEVIN
ABDO Publishing Company

visit us at
www.abdopublishing.com

Published by ABDO Publishing Company, PO Box 398166, Minneapolis, MN 55439.
Copyright © 2012 by Abdo Consulting Group, Inc. International copyrights reserved in all countries.
No part of this book may be reproduced in any form without written permission from the publisher.
The Checkerboard Library™ is a trademark and logo of ABDO Publishing Company.

Printed in the United States of America, North Mankato, Minnesota.
112011
012012

 PRINTED ON RECYCLED PAPER

Cover Photo: Corbis
Interior Photos: Alamy pp. 6, 12, 14, 18; AP Images p. 27; Getty Images pp. 5, 9, 15, 17, 23, 25;
    Glow Images p. 22; iStockphoto pp. 11, 13, 24, 28, 28–29, 29; Neil Klinepier pp. 7, 8, 10;
    Photo Researchers pp. 16, 21; Thinkstock pp. 19, 20–21, 26–27;
    Photo Courtesy of U.S. Army p. 17

Series Coordinator: Megan M. Gunderson
Editors: Megan M. Gunderson, BreAnn Rumsch
Art Direction: Neil Klinepier

Library of Congress Cataloging-in-Publication Data

Kevin, Brian, 1980-
  Guns & ammunition / Brian Kevin.
      p. cm. -- (Gun education and safety)
  Includes index.
  ISBN 978-1-61783-318-2
  1. Ammunition--Juvenile literature. 2. Firearms--Juvenile literature. I. Title. II. Title: Guns and
ammunition.
  TS538.K48 2012
  355.8'25--dc23
                          2011031613

CONTENTS

At the Gun Show

Every year, Evan's dad took him to a gun show. It was a big event for gun collectors. There were exhibits and classes about guns, shooting, and safety. Hundreds of people set up tables where they sold all kinds of guns. Evan saw pistols so small they fit in a pocket and fancy, high-powered rifles. There were even **antique** military guns on display.

At this year's show, Evan's dad allowed him to hold an old six-shooter. Together, they learned about a laser scope. One vendor even showed them how bullets are made.

Yet there was one thing Evan didn't understand. They attended the gun show every year. But his dad never bought anything!

As they headed home, Evan turned to his dad. "How come we never buy anything at the gun show?" Evan's dad thought for a moment. "Sometimes, gun shows are like museums," he said. "Do you take paintings home from a museum?"

Then Evan understood. There are so many different kinds of guns and ammunition. Sometimes the fun part is just looking at them and learning.

Do you want to learn more about old guns, new guns, and different kinds of ammunition? Gun shows are one place people start gathering information.

Guns with long barrels are called long guns. Sometimes they're called shoulder arms, since they're held against the shoulder. Most modern long guns are either rifles or shotguns.

What makes rifles and shotguns different? The **bore** is the main difference. In fact, a rifle takes its name from its rifled bore. That means the walls inside the barrel have shallow, spiral grooves carved into them. These grooves make a bullet spin as it is shot out of the barrel. This spinning motion makes the bullet fly farther and straighter.

Shotguns are often used to hit moving targets such as birds or clay pigeons.

A shotgun is called a smoothbore weapon. The walls inside the barrel are smooth instead of rifled.

Rifles and shotguns also fire different types of ammunition. Rifles fire one bullet at a time. Shotguns usually fire multiple **pellets** called shot. When fired, the shot spreads out and hits a wider area.

Rifles are popular with soldiers, target shooters, and **game** hunters. Shotguns are mostly used for hunting birds. They are also popular for sporting events where participants shoot at clay disks. Sportsmen call these clay pigeons, but they don't look like birds!

**Shotgun
Barrel**

Guns fire bullets, right? That's true, but there's a lot more to ammunition than just bullets. For example, rifles are loaded with small containers called cartridges. The bullet is just one piece of a working cartridge.

A cartridge has four main parts. A metal case forms the outside of the cartridge. It is usually made of brass. The case holds two kinds of explosive powder, primer and gunpowder.

The small cup of primer is just inside the rim of the cartridge. Next to the primer is the gunpowder. A bullet, or **projectile**, sits at the top of the cartridge.

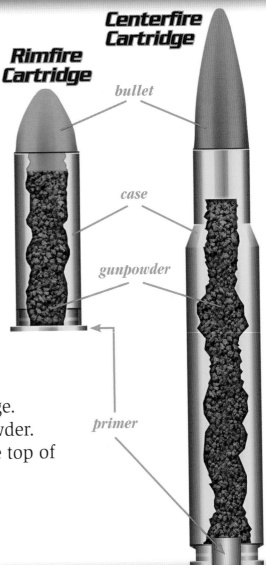

Centerfire Cartridge

Rimfire Cartridge

bullet

case

gunpowder

primer

barrel

cartridge

chamber

firing pin

trigger

Pulling the trigger makes the gun's firing pin strike and **ignite** the primer. The primer ignites the gunpowder. This sends the bullet flying out of the barrel. Without the bullet, the cartridge is spent. So, it is then **ejected** from the chamber.

Most cartridges work this way. They are called centerfire cartridges. However, some cartridges have primer sealed around the entire cartridge rim. These are called rimfire cartridges. The firing pin can strike anywhere on the rim to ignite the primer.

Shotguns use shells instead of cartridges. Shells are similar to cartridges. But, they have five parts instead of four.

Just like a rifle cartridge, everything is kept inside a case. The primer sits at the bottom of the case. Above that rests the gunpowder. A paper or plastic wad comes next. It separates the gunpowder from the shot **pellets** or a **slug**. These sit at the top of the shell instead of a bullet.

Both cartridges and shells are referred to as rounds. Some guns hold just one round. Other guns can hold more. These guns are called repeating firearms. Multiple rounds are held together in a **magazine**. This is not the kind of magazine you read!

Rifle cartridges are measured by their caliber. This measurement also describes the size of a rifle's **bore**. Caliber is measured in millimeters or

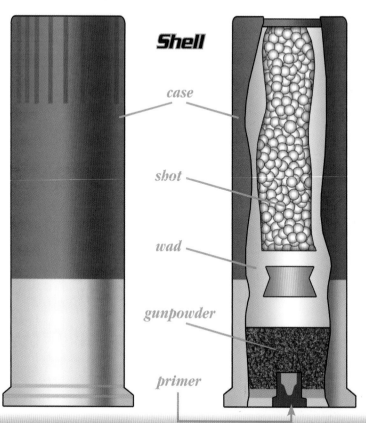

Shell

case

shot

wad

gunpowder

primer

decimals of an inch. The measure of shotgun shells and **bores** is called gauge (GAYJ). A gun's caliber or gauge is stamped on its barrel. This is important information, because using the wrong size cartridges or shells is dangerous!

A magazine may be part of the firearm. Or, it may be a piece that attaches separately.

Loading Long Guns

Pump action

The way a rifle or a shotgun gets loaded depends on the gun's action. This is the **mechanism** that loads, unloads, fires, and **ejects** rounds from the gun. There are five different actions. They are bolt, pump, lever, break, and semiautomatic.

Bolt action

Bolt-action guns have a moveable metal block at the back of the barrel. A shooter pulls a small handle up and back to load a cartridge or shell into the chamber. Moving the handle forward and down again locks the bolt in place. This holds the cartridge or shell in the chamber.

When the bolt is locked, the gun is ready to fire. After firing, moving the bolt again **ejects** the spent round. Then, a new round can be loaded into the chamber.

With pump-action guns, multiple shells can be loaded below the barrel. A pump slides along the barrel. Moving it backward ejects a spent shell. Sliding it forward again loads the next shell into the chamber.

Lever action

Lever-action guns are loaded similarly to pump-action guns. But instead of a pump, they have a long lever. To reload, the shooter bends the lever down and out and then back in.

One famous lever-action rifle was made by the Winchester Repeating Arms Company. Many American pioneers carried a lever-action Winchester. It is sometimes called "the Gun that Won the West."

Break-action firearms fold open on a hinge, like a

door. The back end of the barrel is called the breech. This is where the shooter loads the cartridge or shell. Then the gun is hinged shut. Break-action guns are simple to load, so they are popular for beginners.

Some guns reload themselves after each shot. These have autoloading or semiautomatic actions. Energy from the powder exploding moves the next round into the chamber. Then, the gun is ready to fire again right away.

Break action

Handguns

Like long guns, handguns come in two main types. Pistols are one type of handgun. They have many of the same parts as long guns. There is a barrel and a trigger. A user holds the **stock** of a long gun up to the shoulder. With a handgun, a shooter holds on to the grip.

Handguns are generally carried by police and military forces. But in the United States, private citizens own about 100 million handguns. In Canada, people own approximately 1 million.

Loading a magazine

Most pistols are semiautomatic. A **magazine** loads into the bottom of the grip. When fired, **recoil** helps reload the gun and ready it to fire again. The spent round is popped out of the chamber. And, a new cartridge is pushed into it.

Pistol magazines hold several rounds. So, pistol shooters can fire many times without stopping to reload. Most US police officers carry pistols. Pistols are also popular for target shooting and self-defense.

The 9mm Beretta, or M-9 pistol, has been the standard US military sidearm since 1985.

17

The other type of handgun is the revolver. A revolver also fires multiple rounds. Yet unlike a pistol, it doesn't hold a **magazine**. Instead, a revolver has a spinning cylinder with multiple chambers. When the cylinder rotates, a new cartridge is ready. After firing, the shooter must use an **ejector** rod to remove spent rounds by hand.

There are single-action and double-action revolvers. A single-action revolver must be rotated by **cocking** a small hammer. This lines up a cartridge to fire when the trigger is pulled. A user doesn't need to cock a double-action revolver by hand. Instead, pulling the trigger does this. It both rotates the cylinder and fires the round.

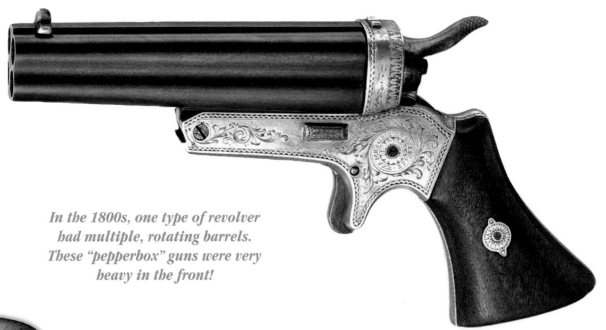

In the 1800s, one type of revolver had multiple, rotating barrels. These "pepperbox" guns were very heavy in the front!

barrel

hammer

ejector rod

cylinder

trigger

grip

Revolvers usually hold six rounds. So, they have been called "six-shooters."

Handgun cartridges are very similar to rifle cartridges. They contain primer, powder, and a bullet in a case. And, they are measured by caliber. A 9-millimeter cartridge fits a 9-millimeter **bore**.

Special Ammo

Gun enthusiasts can purchase many kinds of ammunition at gun shops and sporting goods stores. There is much more to choose from than normal cartridges and **pellet**-filled shells.

Some shotgun shells are loaded with **slugs** instead of shot. A slug is like a large, tapered bullet. Some hunters use slugs when going after larger animals, such as deer.

Other special ammunition includes blanks and dummies. A blank cartridge has no bullet in its case. When fired, the gun only makes a loud noise. So, blanks are good for making sound effects for movies. Dummies contain bullets, but no primer or powder. So, they are simply used to practice loading.

Some police officers use hollow-point bullets. These have an **indent** in the bullet's usually pointy nose. When regular rounds hit hard surfaces, they may **ricochet**. Hollow-point rounds are less likely to ricochet, so they're safer for innocent bystanders.

However, some people do not think hollow-point rounds should be used. When they hit a person, they expand. This is why they don't ricochet, but this also causes more severe injuries. This is one reason hollow-point bullets are not allowed in international warfare.

Hollow point bullets expand when they hit their targets.

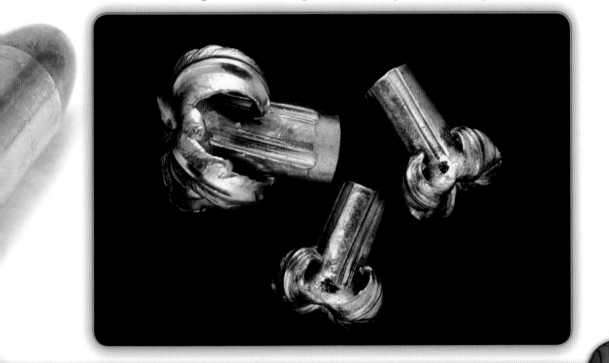

Fire Away!

Whatever the type, all ammunition is **ignited** when a firing pin strikes primer. This process developed from the use of percussion caps, which were first used in the 1800s.

Percussion caps were somewhat like little pills filled with primer. For each shot, a cap was placed near the gun's chamber. The gunpowder and bullet were loaded separately.

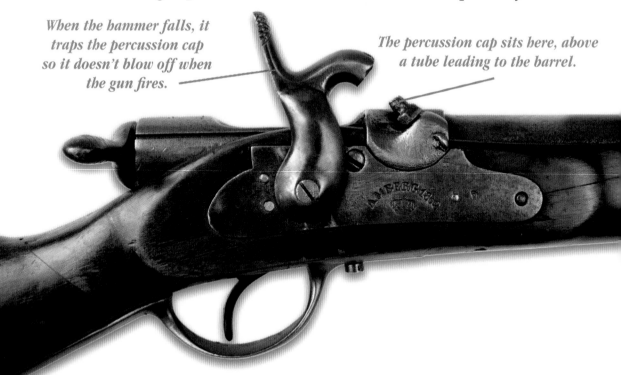

When the hammer falls, it traps the percussion cap so it doesn't blow off when the gun fires.

The percussion cap sits here, above a tube leading to the barrel.

Pulling the trigger caused a hammer to hit the cap. The cap exploded and set off the gunpowder, which **propelled** the bullet from the gun's barrel.

Before percussion caps became widely used, guns had other devices called locks at the breech. The first locks held matches or fuses that were lit by hand. Pulling the trigger on a matchlock gun dropped the match into a pan. The burning match **ignited** gunpowder held there. This ignited gunpowder in the barrel through a small opening called a touchhole.

Lock improvements included wheel locks and flintlocks. These lit the powder with sparks. This occurred when pyrite scraped a metal wheel or flint scraped a bit of steel.

Lead ball ammunition

Most early guns were loaded from the **muzzle**. Powder was poured down the barrel, followed by a lead ball. This was pushed down with a stick called a ramrod. Some sportsmen today still use muzzle-loaders for an extra challenge.

Air Guns

Air guns are popular for recreational shooting and hunting small **game**. There are even Olympic events for target shooting with air guns. These weapons can be just as **accurate** and deadly as regular guns.

Air guns are not technically firearms, because they don't fire due to an explosion. Instead, air guns fire **projectiles** using **compressed** air.

So, an air gun's firing **mechanism** is very different from a regular gun's. A pump or spring traps air under very high

Air gun pellets are shaped like tiny mushrooms or hourglasses.

pressure in a **compression** chamber. Pulling the trigger releases the pressure. This makes the air rush out, which **propels** the ammunition from the barrel.

Unlike typical guns, air guns don't use cartridges. Instead, they use bullets, **pellets**, or darts. Pellets can be fired from smoothbore or rifled air guns. One special type of smoothbore gun fires small, round shots called BBs. BB guns are less powerful than regular air guns.

Automatic Guns

Like semiautomatic guns, fully automatic weapons are self-loading. But there is one major difference. Automatic weapons keep firing as long as the shooter keeps the trigger pulled. They are popularly known as machine guns. Portable types include submachine guns and assault rifles.

An automatic gun's moving parts feed a steady supply of cartridges to the barrel. As in pistols, the cartridges are supplied by a **magazine**. But these magazines can hold many more rounds. The famous Thompson "tommy" submachine guns used by **Prohibition** era gangsters had drum magazines. These saucer-sized cylinders held 50 rounds!

During **World War II**, many varieties of submachine guns were made. Then in 1950, Israeli engineer Uzi Gal invented

Tommy guns weighed nearly 10 pounds (4.5 kg) when empty.

The Uzi has been used by police and military forces in more than 90 countries.

a compact version. The "Uzi" became popular worldwide with police and soldiers.

Today, assault rifles are more common than submachine guns. Assault rifles are special because they are capable of selective fire. That means they have two settings. They can fire one shot, like a standard rifle. Or with the flip of a switch, they can fire automatically like a machine gun.

Owning an automatic weapon requires a background check by the federal government. And, owners must pay a special tax. Automatic weapons are not for hunting or target shooting. Instead, these dangerous firearms are mostly handled by police and soldiers.

Materials

In 600 years of gun history, gun manufacturers have used many materials. Some new guns are made of plastic or metal mixtures called alloys. These guns are lighter and stronger than the metals and woods used in the past.

Collectors have fun finding older guns made from quality materials. Some feature beautifully carved wood. There are many, many different gun designs. No two types are alike.

For people like Evan's dad, a firearm can be a beautiful work of art. Guns and ammunition mix art, science, and technology. Before using them, it is important to understand how these inventions work. But even guns that don't fire are still worth admiring!

Gold, ivory, and beautifully carved wood made older guns works of art as well as weapons.

GLOSSARY

accurate - free of errors.

antique (an-TEEK) - an old item.

bore - the long, hollow inside of a gun barrel.

cock - to pull back the hammer or firing pin of a gun to make it ready to fire.

compressed - stored under pressure in order to have much force when released.

eject - to remove from inside something.

game - wild animals hunted for food or sport.

ignite - to set on fire.

indent - a notch or dent.

magazine - a holder in or on a gun where cartridges are kept before being fed into the chamber to be fired.

mechanism - a system of parts working together.

muzzle - the open front end of the barrel of a weapon.

pellet - a usually round bullet used in shotguns or other firearms that have smooth barrels.

Prohibition - relating to a law banning alcoholic beverages in the United States from 1920 to 1933.

projectile - an object that can be thrown or shot out.

propel - to drive forward or onward by some force.

recoil - the sharp, violent reaction or springing back of a gun when fired.

ricochet (RIH-kuh-shay) - to bounce or skip off a surface.

slug - a type of bullet, or a piece of metal to be fired from a gun.

stock - the usually wooden end of a firearm held against the shoulder for firing.

World War II - from 1939 to 1945, fought in Europe, Asia, and Africa. Great Britain, France, the United States, the Soviet Union, and their allies were on one side. Germany, Italy, Japan, and their allies were on the other side.

To learn more about guns and ammunition, visit ABDO Publishing Company online. Web sites about guns and ammunition are featured on our Book Links page. These links are routinely monitored and updated to provide the most current information available.

www.abdopublishing.com

INDEX